GARRETT AUGUSTUS MORGAN

Businessman, Inventor, Good Citizen

Mary N. Oluonye

authorHOUSE®

AuthorHouse™
1663 Liberty Drive, Suite 200
Bloomington, IN 47403
www.authorhouse.com
Phone: 1-800-839-8640

First published by AuthorHouse 3/28/2008

ISBN: 978-1-4343-4475-5 (sc)

Library of Congress Control Number: 2007907835

Historical pictures by The Western Reserve
Historical Society, Cleveland, Ohio.

Printed in the United States of America
Bloomington, Indiana

This book is printed on acid-free paper.

This book is dedicated to my family for their unwavering support and without whom, this book would not have been possible. Also, a very special thank you to Susan Scheps for reading over my manuscript and for her extremely insightful suggestions. I would also like to thank the very helpful staff of the Western Reserve Historical Society Library, Cleveland, Ohio for their assistance with my research of Garrett Morgan, and the selection of photographs to include in the book. Thank you, All! *–MNO*

GARRETT AUGUSTUS MORGAN

Born: March 4, 1877

Birthplace: Paris, Kentucky

Died: July 27, 1963

EARLY LIFE

Garrett Augustus Morgan was born on March 4, 1877 in Paris, Kentucky, not very far from the state capital of Lexington. His mother was Eliza Reed Morgan. Her father, Reverend Garrett Reed, was Claysville's minister. Garrett Morgan's father was Sydney Morgan, a former slave who had been owned by John Hunt Morgan, a Confederate soldier. Morgan was also Sydney Morgan's father. Sydney Morgan became a free man when Union soldiers killed John Hunt Morgan during the Civil War. Garrett was the seventh of eleven children.

Slavery had ended just twelve years before Garrett Morgan was born, but life was extremely difficult for the newly freed slaves. Suddenly they were free, but they had nothing. They were, for the most part, uneducated, because as slaves, they were forbidden to learn to read and write. They didn't have any money, and they didn't know where to go, or what to do to make a living now that they were free.

The newly freed slaves had so many hopes and dreams for their future. They dreamed of owning land, producing their own food, and making their own money. Owning land meant freedom. But instead, the vast majority of Black people, both in the South and the North, had very little opportunity. Most ended up working as sharecroppers.

Sharecropping was an agricultural system in the South that existed after the Civil War. A White landowner divided his property into several parcels or portions, and then rented out each parcel to a Black family (and sometimes to poor White families). These families were known as sharecroppers. The landowner usually provided a small, primitive cabin for each family to live in. In exchange, the sharecropper family had to farm their parcel of land. Often, the entire family had to work in the fields all day to farm the land. In order to till the soil, grow and harvest crops, they needed equipment, seeds and fertilizer which the landowner supplied to the sharecropper on credit. That meant that the landowner gave the sharecropper what he needed, but the sharecropper would have to pay him back later. At the end of the growing season, the sharecropper would have to give a percentage of the harvest to the landowner. The landowner alone determined how much that percentage would be. The landowner would also tell the sharecropper how much he had to pay him back for the equipment and supplies he had received at the beginning of the growing season. The sharecropper had no choice but to pay whatever the landowner said that he owed.

In the end, most sharecropper families barely made enough to feed themselves. Even worse, they often found that they owed the landowner more and more each year. It seemed that the longer they worked, the more money they owed. They *had* to keep working for the landowner in order to try to pay off all their debts. Most families never did.

GROWING UP

Family life for most Black families living in the rural South after the Civil War was pretty much the same. Most were poor farmers. As soon as children were old enough, they would have to help out on the farm. Garrett Morgan and his brothers and sisters would have started working on the farm as soon as they were about five or six years old. Everybody's help was needed to plow, plant, weed and harvest crops. There were also animals to take care of. The Morgan family grew their own vegetables, and raised pigs, chickens and cows. But life was not all work. With ten brothers and sisters, there was plenty of opportunity to play. Garrett also enjoyed fishing and hunting.

During the time that Garrett Morgan was growing up, most Black children went to school for only two to five months out of the year. The rest of the time they were needed at home to help their parents with the farm work. Garrett was a good farmer, but he preferred to go to school. In fact, he loved school. He attended Branch Elementary School in Claysville. Branch Elementary School was a school for Black children. At that time, Black and White children went to different schools. Schools for Black children in the South were simple one-room buildings with one classroom for all grades – usually first to sixth grades. At Branch Elementary School, Garrett would have learned reading, writing and mathematics. After completing the sixth grade, Garrett graduated from Branch Elementary School. That was the end of his formal education.

MOVING ON

Once Garrett Morgan graduated from elementary school, there were two choices available to him. He could continue to work on the farm. Farming meant back-breaking work, and barely earning enough money to live on after all that work. Most Black farmers remained poor for a lifetime. Garrett's second choice was to look for an opportunity to do more with his life.

A CHANGING COUNTRY

In the mid-1800s, America was beginning to become less of a farming nation, and more of an industrialized one. Inventors such as Alexander Graham Bell and Thomas Edison were amazing the world with their inventions. Bell developed the telephone in 1875, and Edison's inventions included the electric light bulb in 1879.

The development of new machines led to new ways of producing goods. Machines could produce items faster and much more efficiently than they could be made by hand. This led to mass production. Companies could produce large numbers of products in shorter amounts of time. Factories sprung up around many cities across the country, especially in the North, and workers were needed to fill jobs in these factories. Factories offered an opportunity to earn more money, and thousands of people began leaving farms to work in factories in the cities. Cities offered other opportunities besides factory work. In cities, there was greater opportunity for education. There were exciting new tall buildings called skyscrapers to see, and electric lights! There were also immigrants from different countries who brought along with them different cultures and languages.

For a thoughtful, intelligent and curious boy, the pull of opportunity was irresistible.

So in 1891, at the age of fourteen, Garrett Morgan chose opportunity. He said goodbye to his family and to the South, and headed north. He crossed the Ohio River and went on to Cincinnati, Ohio.

THE GREAT
MIGRATION

After slavery was abolished, Black people in the South were still living under slave-like conditions. Treated as less than human, they lived under oppressive and often brutally violent conditions. It wasn't uncommon for a Black person to be killed by White people for the slightest offense. Going North was a chance to escape from all of that. The North had always represented freedom to Black people. Going North meant having a chance to get a decent job so they could take care of themselves and their families. It meant a chance for better education, and a chance to live like a human being with rights.

The migration north began as a trickle. At the time that Garrett Morgan left to go north to Cincinnati, the movement was just beginning. The number of Black people leaving the South would continue to increase dramatically. This movement northward by Black people from the south became known as the Great Migration. By the time it ended in 1940, approximately six million Black people had made the move.

FIRST STOP, CINCINNATI, THEN ON TO CLEVELAND, OHIO

In Cincinnati, Garrett Morgan found a job as handyman for a man who owned property and rented out apartments. Here, he was able to hire a tutor to further his education in English grammar. But a career as a handyman was not what Garrett Morgan had in mind. He saw it as a dead-end job with no opportunity to advance himself. He wanted more, much more. In June of 1895, after nearly four years in Cincinnati, and with ten cents to his name, Garrett moved on once again. He went further north, to Cleveland, Ohio.

When Garrett Morgan arrived in Cleveland, he knew no-one. He had nowhere to stay. For two days and nights he slept outdoors in boxcars in an industrial area of Cleveland. During the day, he searched for a job. Although he was now in the North, Garrett found out that many White people simply would not hire Black people. He was turned away from jobs over and over again. He must have felt very discouraged, but he did not give up. Finally, he got his first job in Cleveland. He was hired as a custodian by Root and McBride Dry Goods Store where he swept the floors for $5.00 a week. Root and McBride Dry Goods Store, which was located in Cleveland's garment district, distributed products such as curtains, floor coverings, blankets, men's clothing and toys. It wasn't long before Garrett moved on to more challenging positions. He worked as a custodian, and then as a sewing machine adjuster at the H. Black Company and L.N. Gross.   Both companies made women's clothing. Garrett always had an inquisitive and thoughtful mind. He was a problem-solver. He liked to study machines in order to understand how they worked, and he thought of ways to make them work more efficiently. While working at the H. Black Company and L.N. Gross, Garrett had plenty of opportunity to observe sewing machines and how they worked. He became well known as a person who could fix sewing machines whenever problems arose. In fact, he devised a belt fastener and other parts for sewing machines which allowed them to operate faster and more efficiently.

When he was nineteen years old, Garrett married seventeen-year-old, Madge Nelson. Their marriage ended in divorce two years later.

A BUSINESS OF HIS OWN

Between 1903 and 1922, Cleveland was one of the most important clothing manufacturing centers in the country. In 1907, after working for twelve years in the clothing business, Garrett Morgan decided that it was time to start his own business. Since he had so much experience repairing sewing machines, it was only natural that he would open up his own shop to repair and sell sewing machines. In 1908, he married again. This time he married a seamstress, Mary Anne Hasek, whom he had met when they both worked at the L.N. Gross Company. Theirs was an interracial marriage. She was White and he was Black. Both families were against the marriage. Mary Anne Hasek's family would not speak to her for a very long time after she married Garrett Morgan. Her parents eventually accepted the marriage, but her brothers never did. However, Garrett and Mary Anne Morgan had a happy marriage. Their marriage lasted fifty-five years and they had three sons. Meanwhile, the sewing machine business was such a success that by 1909, Garrett was able to start another successful business – his own tailoring factory. The factory employed thirty-two workers who manufactured coats, suits and dresses.

Garrett Morgan had come a long way since arriving in Cleveland with only ten cents in

1895. He had two successful businesses, was happily married, and owned his own home at 5202 Harlem Avenue in Cleveland's garment district. He could have been satisfied with that. But Garrett Morgan was always thinking – thinking about the next problem to solve, the next project, the next business, or the next idea.

MORGAN'S SAFETY HOOD

In 1912, Garrett Morgan invented a breathing device to protect firefighters. He had noticed that during a fire, smoke and fumes tend to rise. Therefore, the cleaner air was located near the ground, beneath the smoke and fumes. That observation inspired Garrett to invent an apparatus which he called the Morgan Safety Hood. It consisted of a heat-resistant hood, worn over the head, that connected to two long tubes that joined together mid-way down the back to form one tube. The single tube extended further down, and ended in a bag of clean air, carried in a pouch, or down to the ground where the clean air was. The end of the tube was filled with an absorbent filter, and a valve controlled the flow of inhaled and exhaled air.

For protecting the eyes and lungs in grinding or sand blasting, Morgan's Style Two Helmet cannot be equalled. It affords the workman ample protection without hampering his movements or detracting from his comfort in any way.

Two or four men equipped with Morgan's National Safety Hood can accomplish more in ten minutes of the early stages of a fire than a whole company without such equipment, that is unable to strike the vital point of danger on account of smoke and fumes.

Morgan's National Safety Hood
Style Two Helmet
Combination Smoke, Gas, Ammonia and Sand Blast Protector.

The Morgan Safety Hood allowed firefighters to go into smoke-filled buildings and still be able to breathe. He improved his invention over the next two years, and in 1914, Garrett Morgan received a patent for his Safety Hood. Together with several other Cleveland businessmen, he formed the National Safety Device Company, which made and sold the Morgan Safety Hood. Over the next several years, Garrett Morgan traveled to different states demonstrating how effective the Morgan Safety Hood was. Sometimes he and his assistants would have a fire lit in a canvas tent, making sure that the tent filled with a lot of smoke and fumes. Then a man would put on the Morgan Safety Hood and go into the tent for up to twenty minutes, emerging without any bad effects. He was safe as long as he had the hood on. Unfortunately, in many areas of the country, especially in the

South, Garrett Morgan had to hire White men to do the demonstrations for him. He was afraid that people would not buy the Morgan Safety Hood once it became known that the inventor, (and partner in the business), was a Black man. He was right. Many White people would not buy anything from a Black person, no matter how good the product was.

On July 24, 1916, the Morgan Safety Hood received national attention. Eighty workers at Cleveland Waterworks were constructing a tunnel two hundred and fifty feet below Lake Erie, when an explosion blasted through the tunnel. The tunnel filled with smoke and gas fumes, trapping the men. Two rescue parties that went down into the tunnel to free the trapped men became trapped as well. Ten men died in the process when they were overcome by gas. The situation looked hopeless. Then, someone remembered seeing Garrett Morgan demonstrating the use of his Safety Hood. Cleveland police quickly located Garrett at his home, and asked him to bring along some of his Safety Hoods to the explosion site, to see if there was anything he could do to help the trapped men. When Garrett and his brother, Frank, arrived at the scene, they immediately put on their Safety Hoods. Two other volunteer rescuers put on hoods as well. The four men descended into the smoke-and gas-filled tunnel. There are two stories about what happened next. The most popular version told is that Garrett Morgan, assisted by his brother and two White volunteers, went down into the tunnel over and over again, rescuing a total of thirty-two men, and bringing out some of the bodies of the dead. The second version of the story is that Garrett Morgan, his brother and the two other volunteers went down into the tunnel and rescued two members of the first two rescue parties, then brought up the bodies of ten other would-be rescuers. The actual events may be somewhere in-between. Further rescue was stopped because the United States Bureau of Mines determined that conditions in the tunnel were just too dangerous to permit further rescue attempts.

Unfortunately, Garrett Morgan's contribution to the rescue was not given the acknowledgment that it deserved. Tom Clancy, one of the White volunteers who assisted Garrett, was credited with the dramatic rescue attempt. Clancy was awarded the prestigious Carnegie Medal for heroism and $500.00. Garrett Morgan was terribly hurt and disappointed. He spent several years trying to obtain official recognition of the role he and his brother and the Morgan Safety Hood had played in the rescue. Garrett did, however, receive gold medals from the

Cleveland Citizen's Group and the Cleveland Association of Coloured Men for his heroic rescue efforts.

After the dramatic rescue of trapped workers from the smoke-and gas-filled tunnel, fire departments across the country saw how valuable Garrett Morgan's Safety Hood would be to firefighters who had to enter burning, smoke-filled buildings. Fire chiefs around the country began to buy Garrett Morgan's life-saving Safety Hood.

Meanwhile, World War I had been raging in Europe between 1914-1918. The German Army was using a new weapon – poisonous gases such as mustard and chlorine gas. United States and British soldiers needed gas masks to protect them. The gas masks that were manufactured for the soldiers were similar in many aspects to Garrett Morgan's Safety Hood. So, indirectly, Garrett Morgan helped save the lives of thousands of soldiers during World War I.

Garrett Morgan was a shrewd businessman. He took advantage of opportunity whenever he saw it. Years earlier, in 1905, while working in his home workshop, he had made an accidental discovery which led him to start another business in 1913. He had been trying to find a way to make sewing machine needles stitch more smoothly. He was experimenting with a chemical solution to apply to the needles. When he wiped the solution off his hands with a rag, he noticed later that the curly fibers of the rag had straightened out. Always curious, and always thinking, Garrett Morgan wondered what would happen if he put some of the solution on hair. He happened to own an Airedale – a breed of dog that has curly hair. When Garrett added the solution to the dog's coat, its hair became straight. Next, he tried some of the solution on his own hair. He was not surprised when it straightened his own hair, as well. He wondered what he could do with his new discovery. Since many Black people wore their hair in styles that required straightening their naturally curly hair, Garrett believed that many people would be interested in buying his hair formula. He called his formula, the G.A. Morgan Refining Cream. In 1913, Garrett Morgan the businessman established the G.A. Morgan Hair Refining Company to manufacture and sell his hair-straightening cream. The company also manufactured and sold other hair care products, including a hair dye which was called Black Oil Hair Stain, for men whose hair was turning grey. Once the stain was applied to grey hair, the hair appeared black. Other products were a hair pressing comb for women, hair pressing gloss, hair oil and hair grower. Once again, Garrett traveled across the United States and Mexico, selling G.A. Morgan Hair Refining Company products.

G. A. MORGAN
5204 HARLEM AVE.
CLEVELAND, OHIO
U. S A.

PRESIDENT AND DIRECTOR
  THE G. A. MORGAN HAIR REFINING CO.
GENERAL MANAGER
  THE NATIONAL SAFETY DEVICE CO.
DIRECTOR
  THE CLEVELAND ADVOCATE PUBLISHING CO.

THE CALL

In 1920, Garrett Morgan and a group of men started a newspaper which they named, *The Call*. The newspaper covered news events that concerned the Black community – events that were almost always missing from White-owned newspapers at that time. In 1927, *The Call* merged with another Black newspaper and became, *The Call and Post*.

THE TRAFFIC SIGNAL

Of all of Garrett Morgan's inventions, his most famous was the traffic signal. Two events led to its invention. The first was the increasing use of automobiles in America, thanks to Henry Ford. Henry Ford was another shrewd businessman. When he formed the Ford Motor Company in 1903, he forever changed the way Americans traveled. The Ford Motor Company produced automobiles which many Americans could afford to buy. However, while many Americans began to drive cars, there were still people who walked, used horses and carriages, or rode bicycles to get from place to place. With all those people sharing the roads and using different types of transportation, accidents were bound to happen.

The second event that led Garrett Morgan to invent the traffic signal was an accident that he observed. A car and a horse-drawn carriage crashed into each other. A little girl was badly hurt. Garrett knew that there had to be a better way to keep people safe on the roads. He went home and thought about what could be done. His solution: a three-way traffic sign at intersections to control the movement of traffic in all directions. The year was 1922. The following year, he received a patent for his traffic signal. The G.A. Morgan Safety System, another one of Garrett's companies, described the traffic signal as "a better protection for the pedestrian, school children and R.R. Crossing."

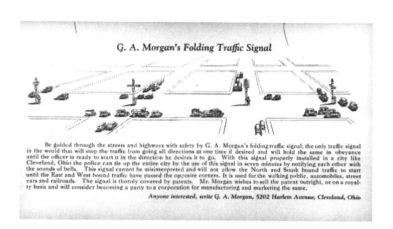

G. A. Morgan's Folding Traffic Signal

Be guided through the streets and highways with safety by G. A. Morgan's folding traffic signal; the only traffic signal in the world that will stop the traffic from going all directions at one time if desired and will hold the same in obeyance until the officer is ready to start it in the direction he desires it to go. With this signal properly installed in a city like Cleveland, Ohio the police can tie up the entire city by the use of this signal in seven minutes by notifying each other with the sounds of bells. This signal cannot be misinterpreted and will not allow the North and South bound traffic to start until the East and West bound traffic have passed the opposite corners. It is used for the walking public, automobiles, street cars and railroads. The signal is thoroly covered by patents. Mr. Morgan wishes to sell the patent outright, or on a royalty basis and will consider becoming a party to a corporation for manufacturing and marketing the same.

Anyone interested, write G. A. Morgan, 5202 Harlem Avenue, Cleveland, Ohio

Garrett was given permission to demonstrate the use of his traffic signal in Willoughby, Ohio. When the General Electric Company heard about his invention, they made an appointment to speak with Garrett Morgan. They saw how the traffic signal worked, and they knew that it was a very good invention. The General Electric Company offered to pay Garrett $40,000 for the patent of the traffic signal. $40,000 was a great deal of money at that time, and Garrett Morgan was happy to sell his patent to the company. He knew that the General Electric Company could do more than his own small company could to ensure that his traffic signal helped a lot of people. Garrett's design for the traffic signal was the initial design for the traffic signals seen on roads all over the country today – signals that control traffic and keep people safe.

GOOD CITIZEN

Garrett Morgan was very involved in the affairs of the Black community throughout his lifetime. He helped form the Cleveland Association of Coloured Men in 1908. The Association worked to improve the economic and social conditions of Black Clevelanders. Later, he joined the National Association for the Advancement of Colored People (N.A.A.C.P.), an interracial organization founded in 1909 by W.E.B. DuBois, with the mission of ensuring equal rights and opportunities for all people. A leader in the

Black community, Garrett Morgan was also a member of the Committee of the Home for Aged Colored People, and the Phillis Wheatley Association – a neighborhood organization that offered social and recreational activities for Black residents. In 1923, Garrett Morgan bought a 121-acre farm in Wakeman, Ohio where he established the all Black Wakeman Country Club.

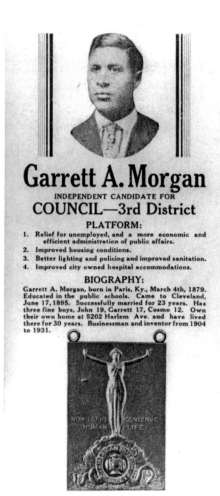

Garrett A. Morgan

INDEPENDENT CANDIDATE FOR

COUNCIL—3rd District

PLATFORM:

1. Relief for unemployed, and a more economic and efficient administration of public affairs.
2. Improved housing conditions.
3. Better lighting and policing and improved sanitation.
4. Improved city owned hospital accommodations.

BIOGRAPHY:

Garrett A. Morgan, born in Paris, Ky., March 4th, 1879. Educated in the public schools. Came to Cleveland, June 17, 1895. Successfully married for 23 years. Has three fine boys, John 19, Garrett 17, Cosmo 12. Own their own home at 5202 Harlem Ave. and have lived there for 30 years. Businessman and inventor from 1904 to 1931.

Local, National and International achievements Mr. Morgan presents to history and science for his race.

Garrett showed an interest in politics, and in 1931, he ran for Cleveland City Council, but he did not receive enough votes to be elected.

LATER YEARS

By 1943, Garrett Morgan had contracted glaucoma, a severe eye disease which eventually destroyed most of his vision. Even though he was losing his sight, Garrett was still thinking of new ways to improve things. In fact, it was during this time, in 1956, that he invented and patented the de-curling comb. He also designed a pellet that could be placed inside a cigarette which would automatically extinguish the cigarette at a certain point if a smoker fell asleep while the cigarette was still burning.

Garrett was growing older and weaker, and he was often sick. He died on July 27, 1963, at the age of eighty-six. He is buried in the historic Lake View Cemetery in Cleveland, Ohio. Other famous people buried in Lakeview Cemetery include, James Garfield, the 20th President of the United States, billionaire and philanthropist, John D. Rockefeller, legendary crime fighter, Eliot Ness, and Adelia Prentiss Hughes, founder of the world famous Cleveland Orchestra.

Garrett Morgan, son of a former slave, who struck out on his own at the young age of fourteen, armed with only a sixth grade education, was a brilliant thinker and a creative problem solver. He was, and still is, a great role model. He demonstrated the importance of having faith and confidence in yourself, of using your mind to conceive ideas, making a plan, and following through on that plan. His ingenuity and inventions have contributed greatly to the safety of generations of Americans.

GARRETT AUGUSTUS MORGAN

Patents

Breathing Device. March 24, 1914.
   Assigned to the National Safety Device
   Company (U.S. 1,090,936 - Official
   Gazette Vol. 200, p. 898)

Breathing Device. October 13, 1914.
   Assigned to the National Safety Device
   Company (U.S. 1,113,675 - Official
   Gazette. Vol. 207, p. 483)

Traffic Signal. November 20, 1923.
   Assigned to Garrett Morgan (U.S.
   1,475,024)

De-Curling Comb. September 18, 1956.
   Assigned to Garrett Morgan

Awards and Citations

1914   Awarded Grand Prize, Golden Medal at the Second International Exposition of Safety and Sanitation

1916   Awarded Medal from City of Erie for bravery in the Lake Erie Disaster

1916   Awarded Medal from Cleveland Association of Coloured Men for bravery in the Lake Erie Disaster

1965   Cited by the U.S. government for the invention of his traffic signal

Other Honors

1967   Plaque in Garrett Morgan's memory placed in Cleveland Public Auditorium

1972   Elementary school in Chicago named in Garrett Morgan's honor

1974   Garrett Morgan's birthplace of Claysville renamed Garrett Morgan Place

1976   A public school in Harlem, New York, named in Garrett Morgan's honor

1991   Garrett Augustus Morgan inducted into the Ohio Science and Technology Hall of Fame

1991   Cleveland Water System's Division Avenue Plant was renamed the Garrett Morgan Treatment Plant in his honor

1994   Students of Boulevard Elementary School in Cleveland Heights, Ohio, raised money to erect a metal plaque at Garrett Morgan's gravesite, paying tribute to his accomplishments

ADDITIONAL RESOURCES

Books

Amram, Fred M.B. <u>African-American Inventors</u>, Mankato, MN: Capstone Press, 1996.

Hayden, Robert C. <u>9 African-American Inventors.</u> Frederick, MD: Twenty-First Century Books, 1992.

Hudson, Wade. <u>Five Notable Inventors.</u> NY: Scholastic, Inc., 1995.

McKissack, Patricia and Fredrick. <u>African-American Inventors.</u> Brookfield, CT: Millbrook Press, 1994.

Murphy, Patricia J. <u>Garrett Morgan: Inventor of the Traffic Light and Gas Mask.</u> Berkeley Heights, NJ: Enslow Publishers, 2004.

Sweet, Dovie Davis. <u>Red Light, Green Light: The Life of Garrett Morgan and his Invention of the Traffic Light.</u> Jacksonville, FL: Evergreen Press, 1978, 1991 printing.

Web Sites

http://www.blackinventor.com/pages/ garrettmorgan.html

http://www.clevelandwater.com/historical/ morgan/garrett_augustus_morganhtm

This will take you to the City of Cleveland Division of Water which provides a biography of Garrett Augustus Morgan.

www.fhwa.dot.gov/education/gamorgan.htm

This will lead you to the Federal Highway Administration U.S. Department of Transportation's article: An American Inventor.

www.nhtsa.dot.gov/kids/townhall/morgan/ morgan2.html

This will take you to the National Highway Traffic Safety Administration's Kid's page and information about Garrett Morgan.

Video

MT Productions/VideoGems. McClendon, W. Stinson, Producer/Director. <u>The Garrett Morgan Story</u>, 1996.

This great video about Garrett Morgan`s life includes interviews with people who knew Garrett Morgan personally, including his grand-daughter, Karren Morgan, his niece, and a business associate.

BIBLIOGRAPHY

Aaseng, Nathan. <u>Black Inventors.</u> New
  York: Facts on File, 1997.

Fiene, Pat, Project Editor. <u>Contemporary's</u>
  <u>Amazing Century Book One 1900-1929.</u>
  Chicago: Contemporary Books, Inc.,
  1992.

Jedick, Peter. "Cleveland's Black Edison."
  Cleveland Magazine, August, 1976: 64-
  70.

Salzman, Jack, Smith, David L., and
  West, Cornel., Editors. <u>Encyclopedia of</u>
  <u>African-American Culture and History,</u>
  <u>Vol. 4.</u> New York: Simon & Schuster
  and the Trustees of Columbia University,
  1996.

Van Tassel, David D., and Grabowski,
  John J., Editors. <u>The Encyclopedia</u>
  <u>of Cleveland History.</u> Bloomington:
  Indiana University Press in association

with Case Western Reserve University,
1987.

Western Reserve Historical Society Library:
Cleveland: <u>Garrett Morgan Papers.</u>

INDEX

K

Kentucky, 1, 6,

L

L.N. Gross, 16, 19
Lake Erie, 24, 44
Lakeview Cemetery, 40
Landowner, 3-4
Lexington, Kentucky, 1

M

Machines, 9
Morgan Safety Hood, 21-27
Morgan, Eliza Reed, 1
Morgan, John Hunt, 1
Morgan, Sydney, 1

N

National Association for the Advancement
    of Coloured People (NAACP), 36
National Safety Device Company, 23,
    30,43
Nelson, Madge, 17
Ness, Eliot, 40

W